A trail guide to walking

THE TEMPLER WAY

from Haytor to Teignmouth

A trail guide to walking the Templer Way:
from Haytor to Teignmouth.

Copyright © Trail Wanderer Publications 2018

www.trailwanderer.co.uk

contact@trailwanderer.co.uk

First Printed 2018

Printed ISBN 978-1-9999509-7-2

By Matthew Arnold.

Editor - Scarlett Mansfield.

Dedication

To Craig & Karolina

Haytor Quarry

TABLE OF CONTENTS

HOW TO USE THIS GUIDE

This guide will provide you with full instructions on walking the entire length of one of the UK's most wonderful long-distance walking paths. The following book is broken down into a number of helpful sections to provide a more enjoyable and detailed experience.

Firstly, an introductory section with background information provides a greater insight into the history and the profile of the terrain you will be traversing over along with the abundance of wildlife that you may encounter.

Secondly, a chapter on preparation will provide all the information you need about reaching the start point, leaving the finishing point, travel information, and distances between each of the major settlements. This enables you to properly plan ahead and make your walk much more enjoyable.

Thirdly, and arguably most importantly, this section provides a detailed description of the whole route - broken down into easily manageable legs. At the beginning of each section, information is provided about accommodation, pubs, and eateries that you will encounter in that section of the walk.

Finally, at the back of the book, you will find a section containing useful information. This includes the contact details and websites of the numerous organisations, groups, and travel information bureaus you may need to ensure your trip runs smoothly.

The Teign Estuary

GENERAL INTRODUCTION

WHAT IS THE TEMPLER WAY?

The Templer Way, named after James Templer, born in Exeter in 1722, links Haytor on Dartmoor with the seaport of Teignmouth. Covering eighteen miles, walkers can enjoy a wide range of scenery, from open moorland in Dartmoor National Park to urban land, estuary shores, woodland, and meadows (to name a few).

The trail somewhat follows the history of the Templer family, hence its name. James Templer, a young runaway, moved to India and made a fortune. Generations of his family consequently profited from this move. His son, James II Templer, built a canal between Teigngrace and the River Teign in England to assist with the transportation of clay in the region. His grandson, George Templer, then built a ten-mile-long granite tramway in the 1820s to export granite from Haytor Down on Dartmoor to his father's canal, the Stover Canal. The tramway track used granite sections to shape its path to guide the wheels of horse-drawn wagons. When the quarry failed to maintain its competitive advantage against Cornish granite, the quarry and subsequent tramway closed in 1858. By 1942, the decline of clay exporting meant the canal ceased to be operational too. Today, the Haytor rocks and quarries are protected as a Site of Special Scientific Interest.

With the exception of open moorland at Haytor Down, the Templer Way is waymarked in both directions. Look out for tramway wheels and the rudder/ tiller of a barge, this is the logo to follow as it represents the aforementioned canal and granite tramway that once flourished in this area.

The Templer Way itself stretches for 18 miles and follows a largely flat surface. The Devon County Council have marked it as a stage-three route meaning it is suitable for wheelchair users and young families. It is not, however, recommended for cyclists owing to the status of land permissions en route.

CHARACTERISTICS OF THE AREA

DARTMOOR

Dartmoor National Park, named after the River Dart running through it, lies entirely in the county of Devon. Set between Plymouth and Exeter, Dartmoor was granted National Park status in 1951; it consequently became a protected area. Prehistoric remains on Dartmoor date back to the Neolithic period, and the area itself contains the largest the largest concentration of Bronze Age remains in the UK.

Dartmoor is steeped in interesting legends, myths, and folklore. Pixies, witchcraft, ghosts, headless horseman, and weird on-goings are rumoured to frequent the landscape. In 1638, rumour even has it that a Great Thunderstorm led the Devil to visit the moorland village of Widecombe-in-the-Moor. Undoubtedly, the thick mist, remoteness, and dark nights contribute to this popular image as the expansive moorland can, at times, appear bleak and desolate. As a result, this haunting scenery has seen Dartmoor inspire a plethora of writers and films. Sir Arthur Conan Doyle's The Hound of the Baskervilles is set in the grounds of Dartmoor, as is James Hewitt's Love and War. When it comes to films, Dartmoor has provided the backdrop for hit movies such as Steven Spielberg's War Horse (2011).

Dartmoor is also home to a training area used by the British army since 1800. After a major prison opened in the area in 1809, soldiers guarding the prison began practising in the area. Over time, troops were drawn to the area owing to the diverse landscape. Today, military training is still carried out by the Navy, Marines, Army and Air Force. Two training camps are located here, and three firing ranges.

It is important to highlight that Dartmoor National Park is the only park in England that allows visitors to wild camp. If you are backpack camping, then the official Dartmoor website states that it is acceptable to do so for one or two nights in some areas of open moorland so long as you stay well away from settlements or roads, and utilise a 'no impact' approach. Please note, preparation and planning are essential in this case as this sort of camping, despite popular belief, is not actually permitted in all areas of Dartmoor.

When it comes to the landscape itself, covering 954km2, Dartmoor is graced with a variety of rivers, bogs, moorland, and hills. Locals often refer to the area as 'The Great Swamp' owing to the erratic nature of the terrain. The highest point, at 621 metres, is the High Willhays and it is, in fact, the highest point in the south of England. For those with an interest in geology, Dartmoor has the largest area of granite in Britain (625 km2). There are also many tors in Dartmoor; these are outcrops of rocks that are the remains of volcanic activity thousands of years ago. There are in fact over 160 hills in Dartmoor with the word tor in their name. Finally, the hilly and often stupendous looking landscape means the park is home to an abundance of walking and cycling routes, suitable for varying levels of fitness.

THE RIVER TEIGN AND THE TEIGN ESTUARY

The River Teign, 31 miles in length, begins its course much like many of Devon's rivers, high up amongst Dartmoor. There are two catchment areas: one located at Teign Head, from where the North Teign river flows eastwards, and another at South Teign. The latter then flows on from Fernworthy Reservoir situated within Fernworthy Forrest. Close to Chagford, the two rivers merge together as one. The river then proceeds onwards, bypassing through the steep sided valley where Castle Drogo is located. Here, it meanders towards and down past the eastern side of the moor, passing Chudleigh, and arriving from the north into and through Newton Abbot.

It is just past Newton Abbot where the river opens up into a broad estuary and leads out in to the English Channel at Teignmouth. The river can still be navigated up to Newton Abbot, although only smaller crafts, less than 2.9m high, can now make this journey due to the construction of Shaldon Bridge.

The estuary provides some wonderful and varied expansive views. Large marshland can be found up until the area that the river opens up, close to Newton Abbot. Intertidal mudflats dominate the area during low tide allowing you to view the winding creeks and the presence of seabirds. At high tide, the area becomes a large expanse of water. On clear days, you can even make out Dartmoor and Haytor from here.

Both sides of the estuary are defined by steep-sided and rounded hills. The north shore provides a busy landscape with the movement from transport links. The A381 runs from Teignmouth to the A380. You can also often see trains hurtling along as the main historic coastal railway that connects Cornwall with the rest of the country runs close to the shore line.

Unlike the northern side, the southern shore provides a more serene atmosphere; secluded and peaceful combes appear alongside sheltered inlets; this area offer a different experience depending on your preferences/ interests.

WILDLIFE & VEGETATION

DARTMOOR

Dartmoor is home to over fifty percent of Britain's population of several globally threatened species. In Devon more widely you can find wonderful birds, butterflies, deer, otters, and horses – to name a few.

The moors are particularly renowned for their butterflies, moths, bees, wasps, dragonflies, and damselflies. The 'All The Moor Butterflies' project has helped to create and restore habitat for several endangered butterflies, from the Pearl-bordered Fritillary to the High Brown Fritillary and the Marsh fritillary; consequently, there are several rare creatures that you may be lucky enough to see for the first time.

There are also many horses on this route that make for an iconic sight on the moors. The Exmoor and Dartmoor ponies are native breeds to the British Isles, and, if you are lucky, you may see some roaming around - many are semi-feral livestock today. Exmoor ponies are considered endangered, and their existence is threatened. Similarly, there are only thought to be around 1,500 remaining Dartmoor ponies in the national park. Written record of the Dartmoor ponies' dates back to 1012 AD; they have had many practical uses over time, especially when transporting granite from the quarry, but today they are more of a cultural landmark and by grazing on the land they help to maintain surrounding habitats and support nearby wildlife.

Other mammals to spot include the famous red deer, a species that has survived on Exmoor since the pre-historic era. Once hunted by the King when the area was designated a royal forest, today it is possible to see calves being born in the months of June and July by the edge of the woodland, or near to the moorland vegetation. Alternatively, if you are very lucky, you might be able to spot an otter in Dartmoor. Once commonplace, a serious decline in the number has led to extreme conservation efforts to enable a comeback. As part of the effort to raise awareness of their demise, you can actually follow an otter trail around the National Park.

TEIGN ESTUARY WILDLIFE

Typically, estuaries provide a less than hospitable environment for animals to live in as changing tides require a certain level of adaptability. In order to see the most wildlife possible, it is best to search the tide times beforehand and consider what season you visit in. The mudflats, however, do offer some wildlife.

Fish are found in abundance therefore the area has always been popular with fishing activities. Species include bass, flounder, grey mullet plaice, salmon and sea trout throughout. You will also find many bird species up and down the estuary that include brent goose, avocet, golden plover and even swans around the closer to the Newton Abbot area.

WEATHER

The best time of the year to walk the Templer Way largely depends on what you hope to see and find. Wildlife flourishes at different times of the year and no one month is particularly better than another unless there is something specific you want to see.

When it comes to temperature, February is the coldest month to visit while July is the hottest. Around nearby Exeter, on average November to April get a high of 10 degrees and a low of 4 degrees Celsius. The weather starts to get warmer in May with an average high of 16 degrees and a low of 7 degrees. Summer really picks up from June to September with average highs of 20 degrees and lows on average of 11 degrees. October is somewhere between, with a high of 15 degrees and a low of 8 degrees.

When it comes to rainfall, the wettest months to visit are from December to March with an average of 30mm of rain every month. April, September, October, and November all average 20mm while May to August averages only 10mm. Overall, January sees the highest average of rain days with 21 days a month, while June sees the least with an average of only 13 days of rain a month.

PREPARATION

ACCOMMODATION

At 18 miles long, the route is fairly short - a person of average fitness would be able to complete the route in one day. However, if you feel like taking a more leisurely approach and taking time to explore more of the surrounding area, you will encounter a multitude of charming hotels, bed and breakfasts, and even campsites to suit all tastes and budgets.

It is impossible to give credit to all of these, however, at the beginning of each leg, you will find mentions of selected accommodation. You can find further contact information under Useful Information on page 59. Stated accommodation will normally be located close to the main trail but you should also remember to account for any added distance it may take.

It is a good idea to spend some time carrying out your own online research to find suitable stopover locations. Websites such as Booking.com and Airbnb also provide a great resource when looking for accommodation. They allow you to reserve a room in someone's home, or guesthouse, at a fraction of the cost of paying for a hotel; great if you plan on staying for only one night.

FOOD & NUTRITION

All of the towns that you will encounter along the Templer Way are situated in close proximity. Refuelling and stocking up on supplies is therefore not going to present much of a problem. However, it is still important to plan for the entire length of your trip so that you have enough calories to sustain yourself; 18 miles is a hefty distance for most.

Ideally, you should consider each leg of your walk and think about what food you are going to need that day to help you complete the distance required. If you are going to be completely self-sufficient then this is one of the fun parts of preparing for the walk as it gives you a chance to be creative, consider what food goes well together, and perhaps even trying things you have not eaten before. You should also consider taking vitamins to supplement any lack of nutrients.

It is a good idea to separate your food into days so you know exactly what you are having on each and do not run out of food faster than expected. If you have allowed yourself extra days for a detour, be sure to account for the energy needed to complete these sections too.

It is also vital to carry enough water to last you for each section. Generally, the route is entirely downhill until you reach Bovey Tracey where the route evens out. Therefore it doesn't present any strenuous effort. But, it is still important to take on enough fluids in order to allow your body to maintain an optimum working temperature, as you will still lose fluids.

If you plan on carrying your own food then make sure you have the lowest weight possible. For example, you should dispose of all food packaging before you depart as this will also rid you of all the litter you would then have to carry around as this is just dead weight. You should also aim to pack light-weight food that is easy to prepare as it will require fewer utensils to do so. If you are worried about a lack of flavour, it may be a good idea to carry small sachets of spices to make meals more exciting.

When it comes to snacks to eat on-the-go, cereal and muesli bars are great options. It is also nice to make your own trail mix. Simply purchase a bag of your favourite nuts, seeds, chocolate chips, and dried fruit and then place them into a small bag to keep on yourself for easy access and energy along the way. All of these can also be eaten separately depending on what resources you have, or that you can find along the way. Other options include rice cakes, chocolate bars, whole-grain tortillas, energy bars, chews or gels.

Again, when it comes to main meals remember to plan in advance. You should ensure that you are taking on a good mixture of complex and simple carbohydrates. For breakfast, porridge oats and wheat flakes with a bit of powdered milk mixed separately would be an ideal option. For dinner, noodles, pasta, and rice make safe, cheap, and light options although remember that rice can take a lot longer to cook. While dehydrated meals and boil in the bags are handy, they are often expensive and use both a lot of fuel and a lot of water. Of course, do not forget to pack instant coffee sachets for a refreshing cuppa to make your walk more enjoyable!

VILLAGE PUBS, SHOPS AND CAFES.

As mentioned, you will pass through large settlements en route and they all offer some form of local amenities such as pubs, cafes, and village shops. You will have many to choose from. Here you can stock up on supplies, or just have a generous meal in one of the pubs. At the start of each section, a number of selected facilities will be listed. Make sure that you account for the time spent in each place as well as the opening and closing time of aforementioned establishments.

The Edgemoor Hotel

NAVIGATION

The trail is a recognised footpath so you will find it marked on OS mapping, below you will find a list of OS maps that you may require. The trail has its own emblem, comprised of a tramway wheel, tiller and a barge's rudder. Apart from the open moorland around Haytor the route is waymarked in both directions.

The scale of a map will depend on how much detail you wish to look at. Even though you can see footpaths on OS Landranger Mapping, OS Explorer maps tend to be more popular with walkers as they offer a greater detail of the terrain therefore I would certainly opt for the 1:25 000.

An example to offer more guidance on scale is in the following example. If you have a map at a scale of 1:25 000, every 1cm represents 25 000cm, in turn equalling to 250m in real life.

OS Explorer Maps are broken down into 4cm gird squares, with each grid square equalling 1km. OS Landranger Maps have 2cm grid squares equalling 1km.

MAPS COVERING THE ROUTE

OS Explorer Maps
1:25 000 Scale
4cm or 1 grid square = 1km

OS Explorer OL28
Dartmoor

OS Explorer OL44
Torquay & Dawlish

OS Landranger Maps
1:50 000 Scale
2cm or 1 grid square = 1km

OS Landranger 191
Okehampton & North Dartmoor

OS Landranger 202
Torbay & South Dartmoor,
Totnes & Salcombe

OS Landranger 192
Exeter & Sidmouth

SIGNPOSTS & WAYMARKERS

Below are some of the examples that you will encounter and should keep a lookout for.

KIT LIST

As with any expedition, planning is of paramount importance, thus compiling a suitable kit list of needed items is an essential task. Narrowing down the items that you need will ensure that you have a happier and safer experience. Depending on the type of outing that you have in mind, whether it be a country ramble, a backpacking holiday, or scaling the largest mountain ranges in the world, you are going to have to create a kit list specific to your expedition.

As mentioned, the Templer Way is roughly 18 miles long, however, it is up to you how long you take to reach the end of your trip. You need to think about how many hours or days you will spend completing each section and prepare your kit accordingly. Below I have provided a kit list that will give you some idea of the equipment that you might want to consider. This is a standard kit list of items that I often take with me on my walks. Of course, you should tailor it to your needs.

You can print this kit list out by visiting
(www.trailwanderer.co.uk/information/kit-list.pdf).

ON PERSON

Item	Notes	✓
Walking boots		
Walking trousers		
Map & Map cover		
Notebook and pen	Keep a note of accommodation on the route.	
Watch	Smart watch to log the route	
Beanie hat		
Buff		
Compass		
£50 / Wallet	Enough cash or transport or supplies.	

PERSONAL KIT CARRIED IN PACK

Item	Notes	✓
Waterproof Liner	A waterproof liner for the inside of the pack	
Sleeping bag		
Bivvy bag		
Roll mat		
Warm kit	Softie down jacket	
Spare socks	4 Pairs	
Spare underwear	4 Pairs	
Towel	Antibacterial towel	
Jet boil / Cooking system	Spare gas	
Hoochie / Tent	Tent pegs	
Bungees	5	
Hydration pack	2 litre	
Spare water	2 litre	
First aid kit	Plasters, deep heat, anti-fungal powder	
Food / Emergency rations	Noodles, boil in the bags, trail mix, nutrition bars	
Lighter/ matches	For lighting cooker	
Gloves		
Hand wipes	Antibacterial wipes	
Survival blanket		
Rubbish bag	For food packaging/general rubbish	

ADDITIONAL KIT

Item	Notes	✓
Spare batteries	3x AAA	
Spare laces		
Flip flops / Light weight trainers		
Portable charger		
Sun glasses		
Thermal mug		
Brew kit	Coffee / Tea sachets	
Multi-tool		
Walking poles		
Head torch		

Teign Ferry

GETTING TO THE START POINT (HAYTOR)

BY RAIL THEN BUS/TAXI

The easiest way to reach the start point is by rail then using a connecting bus service. Newton Abbot hosts a large station and is connected via the main trunk route that runs from Penzance through to London and beyond to the north. Trains frequent the station in both directions approximately every 15 minutes. The station also provides numerous facilities - a cash machine can be found located outside the front of the station too.

Upon arrival at Newton Abbot train station, you will find the bus stop at the front of the station. From here, you can take the Haytor Hoppa bus. The Haytor Hoppa provides a picturesque, circular shuttle service that picks up directly outside the station and drops off at the Haytor Visitor Centre. It is important to note, however, that the service does only run on summer Saturdays, from May until September. The first bus does not depart until 08:55am. Please check operating times prior to traveling, more details can be found from the link below. Note, the Hoppa picks up on the opposite side of the road outside the station.

If you prefer to take a taxi to the start point to set off sooner, then you can find a taxi rank located right outside of the train station to the left of the main building. You can also find a list of local taxi companies under Useful Information on page 60.

(www.dartmoor.gov.uk/enjoy-dartmoor/planning-your-visit/ travel-information/haytor-hoppa)

BY CAR

 You will find a number of car parks around the vicinity of Haytor. You can park at the visitors centre or Haytor's Car Park, situated a few hundred metres further along from the visitors centre. These are owned and managed by the National Park Authority and there is a £2 charge for cars staying over 3 hours. You can also find free laybys and much smaller parking bays within the local vicinity – however, due to the popularity of Haytor these spaces and the carparks can fill up fairly quickly during the summer months so it would be wise to arrive early.

If you decide to drive, you also need to consider how you are going to make it back to the start point to pick up your car once you have completed the trail. There are circular routes possible but of course these routes will add significant time to your walk.

To get to Haytor if you arriving from the north or south, proceed along the A38 and take the slip road signposted for Heathfield. If approaching from the north take the fourth exit. If you are coming from the south take the second exit. Enter on to Newton Road and proceed past Heathfield Industrial Estate on your right. Go straight over at the first roundabout and at the second take the first exit on to the B3387 and follow signs for Haytor. Continue along this road for a further 3 miles until arriving at the Visitors Centre.

More information on parking around Haytor can be found by visiting the following link

(www.dartmoor.gov.uk/enjoy-dartmoor/planning-your-visit/car-parks)

LEAVING THE FINISHING POINT (TEIGNMOUTH)

BY RAIL

Like Newton Abbot, Teignmouth sits on the main rail line; leaving Teignmouth is an easy process. The station also provides many facilities including a cash machine, refreshments, toilets, waiting rooms, and a ticket booth.

Trains serve the station roughly every 10 minutes with most running between Exmouth and Paignton. However, connections onwards to further destinations can be made from either Exeter or Newton Abbot.

BY CAR

If you decided to leave your car in Haytor, you can follow the instructions from the 'getting to the start point' in reverse. Simply get the train Newton Abbot and then bus to Haytor.

If you plan on getting picked up at the end point, it is very easy to find. Numerous car parks can be found in the area too. If you are arriving from the north, merge onto the A380 from the M5. After roughly 18 miles take the slip road, following signs for Teignmouth.

If you are arriving from the south make your way up the A38 and take the Drumbridges exit, signposted for Newton Abbot. Take the fourth exit onto the A382 and follow the road leading into Newton Abbot. At the arrival of a mini roundabout take the first exit onto Jetty Marsh Road. At the next roundabout take the third exit continuing along Jetty Marsh Road. Again, at the next roundabout take the first exit on to Newton Road, continue straight passing the Tesco superstore on your left and at the mini roundabout take the second exit right, on to Greenhill Way. Follow the road round until you meet up with the A383 and at the roundabout take the second exit. At the A380 turn off continue straight over to join on to Teignmouth Road (A381), which after 3.7 miles leads into Teignmouth.

BY BUS

If you feel that getting away would be more convenient by bus then you have the choice of routes 2 and 2B these both run between Exeter and Newton Abbot where you can then get a connection to onwards travel or additional services to either up or down the country.

Teignmouth is also a stop for the National Express Routes 337 - Rugby to Paignton and the 501 - London and Plymouth.

DISTANCE CHART

Templer Way	Km	Miles	Elevation Gain
Haytor - Bovey Tracey	8.1	5	34
Bovey Tracey - Newton Abbot	10.5	6.5	50
Newton Abbot - Teignmouth	10.3	6.4	73
Total	**28.9km**	**18m**	**162m**

The mileage chart, shown above, is useful to indicate the distance between each of the major settlements on route. As well as this, the chart also shows the expected elevation gain within each leg of the walk.

You can see from the elevation chart below that there is barely any incline and that the route is entirely downhill from the high start point until it levels out after Bovey Tracey.

HIGHT ELEVATION CHART

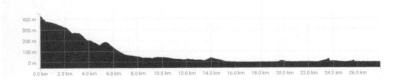

Please note: All figures given are approximations, these distances and elevation will vary based on diversions.

Templer Way
Haytor - Teignmouth

THE ROUTE

Devon

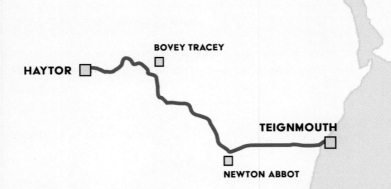

HAYTOR

BOVEY TRACEY

TEIGNMOUTH

NEWTON ABBOT

LEG 1 - HAYTOR TO BOVEY TRACEY

Haytor Rocks

Haytor

OS Grid Ref: SX 760 774
District: Teignbridge
OS Explorer map:
OL28 - Dartmoor

Leg Distance: 8.1 km / 5 miles
Elevation Gain: 34 m

Points of interest
National Park Visitor Centre
Haytor Quarry
Haytor Car Park
Saddle Tor Car Park

Accommodation & Eateries
Tinpickle And Rhum
The Rock Inn
Haytor Barns
Bramley Wood B&B

Bus Station
193 - Bovey Tracey to Newton Abbot
Haytor Hoppa - Newton Abbot to
Manaton

25

IMPORTANT

An important point to note, that you should factor into your walk if you plan on taking the final ferry from Shaldon to Teignmouth, the last ferry trip commences 15 minutes before the finishing time. Times do vary depending on the time of year, so it would be worth checking the timetable beforehand. If you do not manage to reach the ferry in time, you can reach Teignmouth by crossing over Shaldon bridge.

More details on ferry times can be found from the link below
(www.teignmouthshaldonferry.co.uk)

Located on the eastern edge of Dartmoor National Park, Haytor also known as Haytor Rocks or Hay Tor is a formation of large granite rocks. It is one of the most popular spots on Dartmoor and it is easy to why, with a height of 457 metres it offers truly remarkable views across Dartmoor and the surrounding countryside towards South Devon's Coast, even towards the estuary where the finishing point is located.

The start point provides a number of facilities. The visitors centre is a particularly great place to find out more information about the area including wildlife leaflets and additional things to do – it's also possible to pick up a memento from here. The Visitors centre can be found at the base of hill leading up to the tor. Toilets and a car park are also located next to the centre. Authorities have also recently introduced parking fees to raise money to maintain the area; it is £2 for all day parking and charges apply between the hours of 10:00 am - 6:00pm daily.

A short distance walk, to the right of the Visitors Centre, is the hamlet of Haytor Vale. You will find Tinpickle And Rhum and the Rock Inn as well as a number of B&Bs.

The northern slopes of Haytor Down have a long standing history with quarrying. However, it was not until the nineteenth century that companies worked the area commercially. Located near to the main granite tors you can also find the long disused Haytor Quarry. Historically, builders used Haytor granite across towns and cities across England. It was even used in the reconstruction of London Bridge, opened in 1831. In 1919, the last rock was quarried here and used in the Exeter War memorial. Today, the quarry simply provides a wind-sheltered walk around the small lake within.

If you are ready to begin the trail, if you have not already, proceed the short distance over to Haytor Quarry and head around to the north-east side from where you will easily be able to distinguish the granite track bed.

The start point is marked by a large granite stone with the familiar Templer Way waymarker imprinted into it. This can be found at the Y intersection where the granite trackway leads off towards Haytor Quarry and merges into the track that continues on further to the north.

Head downhill in the direction of the trackway until you arrive at the small road that leads off from the B3387. At the road, cross straight over and continue to follow the trackway, a prominent feature on the ground during this section of the route. Coming down from Haytor Down provides a wonderful view out towards the estuary in the far distance. On a clear day, you will be able to make out the high ground of Shaldon, the final settlement where the ferry crossing to Teignmouth is located.

Here, the trail meets up and runs alongside the B3387, the main road between Bovey Tracey and Widecombe in the Moor, passing through Haytor.

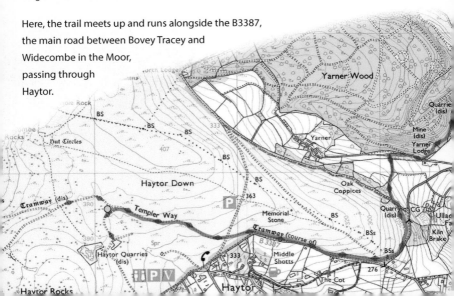

Yarner Wood Trackbed

View Looking out from Yarner Wood

Yarner Wood

The 365 acre woodland lies on the eastern point of Dartmoor and today makes up part of the East Dartmoor Woods and Heaths National Nature Reserve. The woodland is home to many different types of tree - oak, birch, larch, beech and scots pine, to name a few. It also attracts a vast array of birds such as buzzards, sparrow hawks and nightjars.

The woodland also has a long history of human activity; it is possible to trace the first mention of the woods back to sixteenth century. Between 1857 and 1862, for example, a copper mine, employing between 40 and 50 men, operated within the woodland. The ruins of Yarrow Mine are still visible today.

Proceeding along the path, you will notice it eventually arcs round to the left at the base of the high ground to your left. Eventually, the path joins up with a bridleway that runs horizontally across. Here, you will leave the open moorland behind and proceed along a permissive path that leads on through and into the south-eastern corner of Yarner Wood.

Whilst passing through Yarner Wood you will eventually meet up with the old granite track bed again as it curls through the south-eastern boundary of the woodland. This area actually provides the best view of the track bed. This section also provides a number of seated areas offering snapshots through the clearing of the beautiful views beyond.

Upon arrival at the gate, pass through and leave Yarner Wood behind.

Continue straight as the trail leads down and joins up with a bridleway at Lower Down. At the time of writing, when you reach the bridleway, a diversion is in place – the path straight ahead is currently closed off to the public. Instead, turn right and head upwards along the bridleway to arrive at the B3387.

At the main road, turn left and proceed downhill for approximately 1 km to the crossroads where The Edgemore Hotel is located. Please note, the B3387 is a fairly busy road as it is the main route up to Haytor from Bovey Tracey, do take extra caution in this area.

At the cross roads, turn right onto Chapple Road, a bench offering respite can be found on the right-hand side. Proceed downhill. After a short distance, enter into the wooded area on your right. Pass through the woodland and enter out back onto Chapple Road and follow round to the right. Before the next bend, over to your right you will see the only remaining bridge that the tramway used to cross – known as the Bovey Pottery Leat.

Proceed over the small granite bridge and pass along the trackway to once again be brought out onto Chapple Road. Take the left track leading off from Chapple Road and proceed along until you are brought out at Brimley Road. Cross straight over onto Shaptor View and continue straight onto Pottery Road, eventually by-passing Pottery Pond on your left.

You will now be located in the southern-most residential area that makes up the first major settlement on the trail, Bovey Tracey.

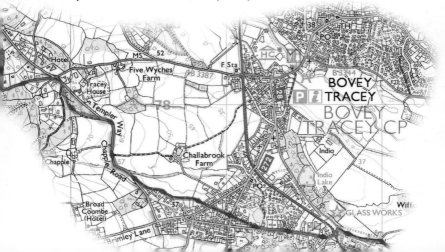

LEG 2 - BOVEY TRACEY TO NEWTON ABBOT

Fore Street, Bovey Tracey

Bovey Tracey

OS Grid Ref: SX 810 772

District: Teignbridge

OS Explorer map:
OL44: Torquay & Dawlish

Leg Distance: 10.5 km / 6.5 miles

Elevation Gain: 50 m

Points of interest

Dartmoor Pony Heritage Trust

Dartmoor Whisky Distillery

House of Marbles

St Peter, St Paul & St Thomas' Church

Accommodation & Eateries

Home Farm Café

Brookside Café & Restaurant

The Edgemoor Hotel Dartmoor

The Devon Guild of Craftsmen

Cromwell Arms

Courtenay House - B&B

Bus Station

39 - Exeter to Bovey Tracy

Haytor Hoppa - Newton Abbot to Manaton

Bovey Tracey is a small town located close to the edge of Dartmoor with a history that can be traced back to the Saxon period. Interestingly, the town is home to over one hundred listed buildings, with the most prominent being the parish church located at the top of the town. Bovey Tracey is named after the River Bovey as the river flows south of the town. Although the first mention of the name appears in the Domesday book as Bovi, the Tracey part of the name comes from the Tracey family who became rulers after the Norman Conquest. The first mention of the town as 'Bovitracy' dates from 1309 onwards; it has evolved since then.

During the English Civil War, even Oliver Cromwell visited the town. Parliamentarian troops entered the city after dark and caught a group of Lord Wentworth's regiment. A battle subsequently took place the next day on Bovey Heath.

On this walk, you will first arrive in the southernmost part of Bovey Tracey, approximately 1.8 km from the town centre. If you feel up to the extra walk and have an interest in exploring the town then you can reach it by turning right at Pottery Road, proceeding straight, then left on to Ashburton Road. Here, continue straight until you reach a junction. Proceed onto Newton Road and follow it around onto Station Road which merges into Fore Street and to the centre where you will find many shops, eateries and pubs.

If you do not feel up to a walk then continue a few metres along Pottery Road and head left - you will find the House of Marbles with the Old Pottery Restaurant.

To continue the trail, proceed left to the very end of Pottery Road. Upon arrival at the roundabout, make your way to the opposite

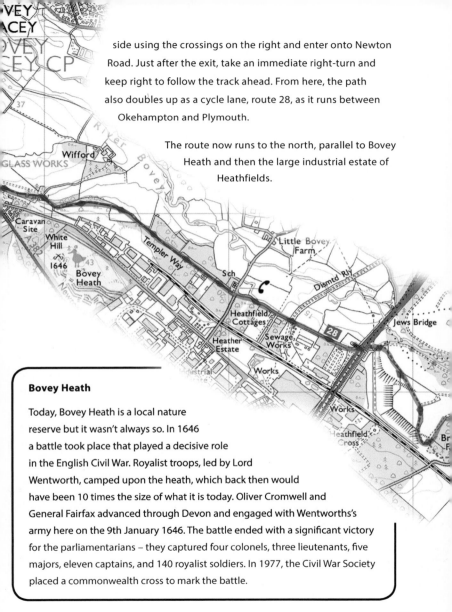

side using the crossings on the right and enter onto Newton Road. Just after the exit, take an immediate right-turn and keep right to follow the track ahead. From here, the path also doubles up as a cycle lane, route 28, as it runs between Okehampton and Plymouth.

The route now runs to the north, parallel to Bovey Heath and then the large industrial estate of Heathfields.

Bovey Heath

Today, Bovey Heath is a local nature reserve but it wasn't always so. In 1646 a battle took place that played a decisive role in the English Civil War. Royalist troops, led by Lord Wentworth, camped upon the heath, which back then would have been 10 times the size of what it is today. Oliver Cromwell and General Fairfax advanced through Devon and engaged with Wentworths's army here on the 9th January 1646. The battle ended with a significant victory for the parliamentarians – they captured four colonels, three lieutenants, five majors, eleven captains, and 140 royalist soldiers. In 1977, the Civil War Society placed a commonwealth cross to mark the battle.

Stover Canal Graving Dock

Footpath Leading Towards Town Quay

When you arrive at the crossroads, continue straight ahead. Here, the route proceeds past Heathfield cottages and further on past the water treatment works on your right-hand side. Continue along this road until you are brought to the edge of the busy A38, also known as the Devon Expressway. Once here, use the walkway and bridge to your left to cross over to the opposite side of the road.

Once on the other side, you will be now located in front of another wildlife habitat, the Teigngrace Meadow Nature Reserve, created from the diggings of nearby quarries. Birds and butterflies can be found in abundance through the meadowland and steep slopes.

For ease, you can follow the hard-standing cycle path where you will join up with the country lane at Brocks Farm. Otherwise, you can proceed right and into the meadow then pass over the top of the reserve where you will arrive at the west side of Brocks Farm. From here, follow the track around to be brought out at the same corner where the cycle path and road join.

From where you join the narrow country lane, proceed left keeping to the road. It eventually bends right then round to the left. Continue on and pass Ventiford Cottages on

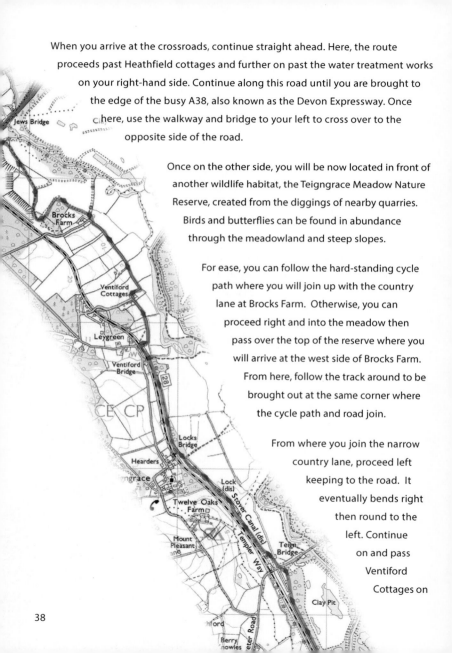

your left as the road merges into Summer Lane. Follow along Summer Lane until you round a corner - pass underneath the railway bridge and, at the junction, turn left. Take the next left into the driveway and pass back underneath the railway bridge to the opposite side again. Once you have passed the bridge you will be now situated at Ventiford Basin.

Stover Canal and Ventiford Basin

The Ventiford basin is the northernmost point of the Stover Canal. James Templer began constructing the 1.7 mile long canal, along with its five locks, in 1790.

Workers brought clay from the surrounding areas to this point to load the product onto waiting barges. Once full, the 50ft barges, laden with 20 tons of clay, would travel down to the Jetty Marsh sea lock navigating through all five locks. Depending on the tide, barges would then continue onwards along the Whitelake channel past Town Quay, located in Newton Abbot, and down the river Teign. From here the cargo would be transferred to larger ships waiting at Teignmouth docks.

In 1820, James Templer II's son, George, built the Granite Tramway using granite from the quarries of Haytor so supplies of the product could follow the same route.

It was not until the arrival of the railway in 1866 that the canal basin became redundant. Activity, however, still remained up until 1937 when it finally ceased and started to fall into disrepair. At the end of the fourteen year lease in 1942, the canal was finally abandoned. Subsequently, over the following years, flooding by the nearby river Teign caused layers of silt to build and eventually buried all evidence of the canal.

Today, after many excavations and numerous surprises, interested parties rediscovered the historic canal. It is now managed by Stover Canal trust who work closely with the local council and other parties to preserve the canal. Plans are even in place to restore Ventiford basin to provide an attractive rest area for tourists and local residents.

Leading off from the basin, the path now follows along the tow path that once ran beside the canal. Much of the path is lined by trees and you can still make out the channel where the canal would have been, although it is now completely overgrown. The next significant point you will arrive at is Locksbridge located at the village of Teigngrace. Locksbridge is the first lock leading in the direction of the Teign Estuary; it was built using the granite quarried from Haytor.

From Locksbridge the trail continues to follow alongside the overgrown canal channel as well as the train line that runs parallel. Upon reaching the boundary of the clay works, you will now be situated in another local nature reserve, the Jetty Marsh Basin, part of the River Teign flood plain. Pass back over to the opposite side of the railway line and proceed onwards to enter out at the roundabout located in front of Newton Abbot's fire station.

Town Quay Marker Stone

LEG 3 - NEWTON ABBOT TO TEIGNMOUTH

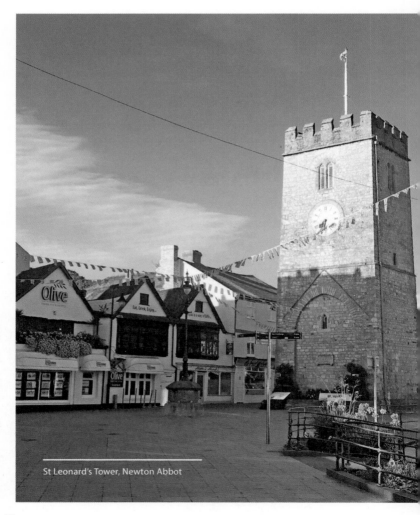

St Leonard's Tower, Newton Abbot

Newton Abbot

OS Grid Ref: SX 863 717
District: Teignbridge
OS Explorer map:
OL44: Torquay & Dawlish

Leg Distance: 10.3 km / 6.4 miles
Elevation Gain: 73 m

Points of interest

St Leonard's Tower
Decoy Country Park
Courtenay Park
Newton Abbot Town and GWR Museum
National Trust - Bradley
Ye Olde Cider Bar

Accommodation & Eateries

Mackenzie's Diner
The Clock Tower Coffee Shop
Mad Hatters Cafe
Coffee#1 Newton Abbott
Luffs Cafe
Courtenay House - B&B
Hazelwood Guest House
The Union Inn
Premier Inn Newton Abbot

Bus Station

2 - Exeter to Newton Abbot
Gold - Plymouth to Torquay, change at Totnes
501 - National Express London to Plymouth
Haytor Hoppa - Newton Abbot to Manaton

To reach the town centre from where you came out at the roundabout, next to the fire station, proceed along The Avenue. After the bend, continue straight until you are brought to the crossroads where Queen Street runs horizontally.

To press on with the trail, at the roundabout take the left track that leads down and behind the National Tyres and Autocare garage. From here, the path runs behind a small industrial estate and alongside an overflow section of the River Teign. You should eventually enter out onto a grassy area. Follow the path round to the right. Head up and over the small foot bridge that crosses the River Lemon. At the other side, turn left and pass under the large railway bridge to be brought out at Town Quay, a historic docking area associated with the clay, timber, coal and of course granite trade that used to pass through here before heading on to Teignmouth. You will also find a welcome refreshment kiosk, a great place to recuperate and take in the views of the marshes and Teign River.

Leading off from the Kiosk, follow the road right onto Forde Road then take the next left. Continue straight through another small industrial estate as the road merges into Collett Way, keeping a look out for a path on your left. Follow the path to re-join alongside the bank of the River Teign. Proceed straight and cross over the walkway to the opposite bank. Here, turn left and continue to follow the bank, passing underneath the large bridge that carries the A380.

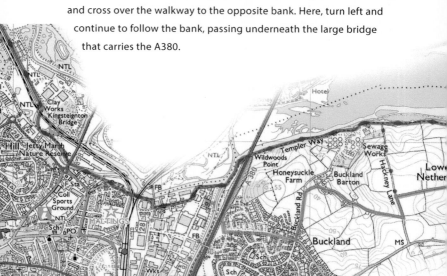

The River Teign

Looking over to the Northern Shore

Looking towards Shaldon Bridge

! Warning !

A very important point to note, on the opposite side of the A380 bridge, the trail continues alongside the bank of the estuary and is only accessible during low tide. Please check tide timings before commencing onwards and leave enough time, at least 2 hours within low tide, before pressing onwards along this part of the route. If in doubt, an alternative route can be made via a diversion, found on the next page.

More information on tide timings can be found by visiting the link below.
(www.tidetimes.co.uk/teignmouth-approaches-tide-times)

Providing that the river bank is accessible, proceed onwards alongside the bank. Take care on this next section as the ground can be incredibly slippery and wet with seaweed littered about the path. Opposite the sewage treatment plant you will find access to a road, Hackney Lane, that leads up to join onto Shaldon Road. This point provides a fantastic view down the estuary of the north side.

DIVERSION

If the water is at high-tide and you wish to follow the diversion, where the path enters along the bank of the estuary, turn right and proceed up the path that runs alongside the A380. You will eventually appear level with the dual carriageway.

Continue along the path until you enter out in front of a park located at the west of the Buckland housing estate. Lead off left and proceed up Chichester Way. Take the fourth left onto Buckland Road and keep following the road, heading past the Mare & Foal Sanctuary on your left. Continue until you arrive at the T-junction.

At the junction, turn left then take the next right and proceed along the road passing through Lower Netherton. At the crossroads, continue straight and join onto Shaldon Road. At Combeinteignhead, follow the road around to the left and continue along Shaldon Road. At the first left you can find the road that leads down to the Coombe Cellers, a pub providing food and fantastic views up and down the Estuary. Otherwise, to reach Shaldon, continue along Shaldon Road. At Devon Valley Holiday Village, continue straight along Coombe Road for the remainder until you arrive at Shaldon.

Continue onwards along the shore, keeping close to the bank. Do not be tempted to take a short cut across the mud flat at the point in where the bank cuts into the right as you could become stuck. Your next point of call will be The Coombe Cellars Pub & Restaurant, a place that used to be used for fishing and smuggling. Today, providing good food and drink, it is a great place to recuperate; you can sit out on the decking and enjoy more spectacular views of the estuary.

To press on, at the entrance to the car park, pass down the slip road and continue along the southern shore, again keeping close to the bank. Upon passing Hearn Field and houses close to the edge, you will join up with Shaldon Road where you will briefly round a corner on the road to enter back onto the path along the estuary. Once round the next corner, you will be presented with a clear view of the finishing line as well as the bridge that connects Shaldon and Teignmouth.

After you have passed the holiday camp, pass round the final corner and proceed by the houses on your right and enter up the slip way onto The Strand. Proceed to the end and turn left onto Ringmore Road. At the first left, proceed down the narrow road in-between the houses and go to the edge of the river once more. Benches are positioned over to your left and offer another perfect spot to sit down and take in the views of the estuary.

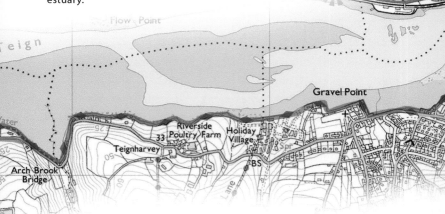

Continue right as you lead down to Shaldon Bridge. Upon reaching the bridge, it is at this point that you can complete the remainder of the trail by passing over Shaldon Bridge and following the road around to the right, down in to Teignmouth, if you think you may not make the ferry.

Otherwise, at the start of the Shaldon Bridge, continue directly straight, bypassing Saint Peter the Apostle church, and follow the road around to the right onto Albion Street. At the first left, proceed onto Riverside and keep following the road all the way down to the Clipper Café to be brought out on the Strand. Here, settled amongst the beautiful tiny seaside cottages, you will encounter more places to eat. As you proceed down along the Strand keep a look out on your left, situated next to the post box, for a small hut. Here you will find the ferry waiting area. The ferry embarks a few metres from the shore so be sure to keep a look out for it.

Once you have made the 10-15 minute crossing you will be situated at Teignmouth's so-called back beach. Proceed straight, up along Lifeboat Lane. Turn right and then head left through the car park where you can finish the remainder of the path along the South West Coast Path, passing Teignmouth Lighthouse, until you arrive at Teignmouth's seafront and grand pier.

FINISHING AT TEIGNMOUTH

Teignmouth Back Beach

Teignmouth

OS Grid Ref: SX 943 729

District: Teignbridge

OS Explorer map:
OL44: Torquay & Dawlish

Points of interest
Teignmouth Lighthouse
Grand Pier
Train Station
Teignmouth Back Beach
Public Car Parking
Eastcliff Park
Pavilions Teignmouth

Accommodation & Eateries
Crab Shack
The Old Java Coffee House
The View Bar & Cafe
The Hobbit
East Cliff Cafe
TwentySix
Ye Olde Jolly Sailor Inn
The Thornhill B&B
Cliffden Hotel
Lynton House Hotel
Brunswick House B&B

Buses
2, 2B - Exeter to Newton Abbot
22 - Dawlish to Paignton
122 - Tavistock to Dawlish
501 - National Express London to Plymouth

Teignmouth, known as the gem of South Devon, is a large seaside town and fishing port home to nearly 15,000 residents. Situated on the north bank of the estuary of the River Teign, thousands of visitors come to enjoy all the town has to offer each year.

Historically, owing to its status as a port, foreign countries frequently targeted Teignmouth. After an invasion by the French in July 1690, Teignmouth became the last place in England to be invaded by a foreign power. Soldiers destroyed much of the town and the crown, as a result, issued a church brief that collected £11,000 to help repair it.

The town grew rapidly from the nineteenth century onwards – once a mid-sized fishing port associated with the Newfoundland cod industry, Teignmouth became a fashionable tourist resort. The 1846 opening of the South Devon Railway helped speed up this process. A year later, the pier was built; it remains a crowd-pleasing attraction to this day as it is one of only two piers left on the south-west coast of England.

Sadly, World War One devastated the town. Many men lost their lives and businesses struggled. However, these woes did not last for long. By the 1930s, the town made a comeback and returned to its former glory.

Today, though not as popular as it once was, Teignmouth remains a frequented and much-loved destination in Devon. Popular attractions in the area include a visit to Ness Cove, Shaldon Wildlife Trust Centre, or to the Old Walls Vineyard nearby.

Teignmouth is also the start point of many other both short and long-distance walks. Once you have finished the Templer Way, if you are still wanting more you could complete the Teignmouth to Dawlish Railway Walk. Alternatively, you could begin the South West Coast Path from here. Though the path officially starts in Poole Harbor, it passes through Teignmouth. This route, however, is not for the faint-hearted – at 630 miles long, it is the longest National Trail in the whole country! Alternatively, if you are finished exploring for the day, you can make your way home easily using the information provided on page 19.

Relax! You have now finished this walk and have earned a well-deserved rest.

Grand Pier, Teignmouth

USEFUL INFORMATION

ORGANISATIONS

Visit Dartmoor
Web: www.visitdartmoor.co.uk
Facebook: @VisitDartmoor
Twitter: @visitdartmoor

Visit Devon
Web: www.visitdevon.co.uk
Facebook: @VisitDevon
Twitter: @VisitDevon

Teignbridge District Council
Web:www.teignbridge.gov.uk
Facebook: @Teignbridge
Twitter: @Teignbridge
Email: info@teignbridge.gov.uk

English Heritage
Web: www.english-heritage.org.uk
Facebook: @englishheritage
Twitter: @EnglishHeritage
Phone: 0370 333 1181
Email: customers@english-heritage.org.uk

Stover Canal
Web: www.stovercanal.co.uk
Email: info@stovercanal.co.uk

National Trust
Web: www.nationaltrust.org.uk
Facebook: @nationaltrust
Twitter: @nationaltrust
Phone: 0344 800 1895
Email: enquiries@nationaltrust.org.uk

Ramblers
Web: www.ramblers.org.uk
Facebook: @ramblers
Twitter: @RamblersGB
Phone: 020 7339 8500
Email: ramblers@ramblers.org.uk

Haytor Visitors Centre
Web: www.dartmoor.gov.uk/
enjoy-dartmoor/planning-
your-visit/virtual-visitor-centre/
haytor-visitor-centre
Phone: 01364 661520

Long Distance Walkers Association
Web: www.ldwa.org.uk

COMMUNITY INFORMATION

Haytor
Web: www.dartmoor.gov.uk/
enjoy-dartmoor/places/haytor

Bovey Tracey
Web: www.boveytracey.gov.uk

Newton Abbot
Web: www.newtonabbot-tc.gov.uk

Shaldon
Web: www.shaldon-devon.co.uk

Teignmouth
Web: www.newtonabbot-tc.gov.uk

PUBLIC TRANSPORTATION

National Rail Enquiries
Web: www.nationalrail.co.uk
Phone: 03457 48 49 50

National Express
Web: www.nationalexpress.com/en
Phone: 0871 781 8181

First Bus
Web: www.firstgroup.com/somerset
Phone: 0345 602 0121

Interactive Devon bus routes
Web: www.traveldevon.info/bus/
interactive-bus-map/

Traveline
Web: www.traveline.info
Phone: 0871 200 2233

Stagecoach
Web: www.stagecoachbus.com
Email: southwest.enquiries@
stagecoachbus.com
Phone: 01392 42 77 11

Haytor Hoppa
Web: www.dartmoor.gov.uk/enjoy-
dartmoor/planning-your-visit/
travel-information/haytor-hoppa

Teignmouth to Shaldon Ferry
Web: www.teignmouthshaldonferry.co.uk
Phone: 07896 711822 Or 07940 503314

SELECTED EATERIES

Tinpickle And Rhum
Web: www.tinpickleandrhum.com
Phone: 01364 661407

The Rock Inn
Web: www.rock-inn.co.uk
Phone: 01364 661305

Home Farm Café
Web: www.homefarmcafe.co.uk
Phone: 01626 830016

Brookside Café & Restaurant
Web: www.brooksiderestaurant.co.uk
Phone: 01626 832254

The Devon Guild of Craftsmen Cafe
Web: www.crafts.org.uk
Phone: 01626 831959

Mackenzie's Diner
Web: https://www.facebook.com/
pages/biz/diner-newton-abbot/
Mackenzies-Diner-354985167949250/
Phone: 01626 331529

Mad Hatters Café
Web: www.spongeinthemiddle.com
Phone: 01626 337666

The Clock Tower Coffee Shop
Web: www.facebook.com/
Clocktowercoffeeshop
Phone: 01626 332194

Luffs Café
Web: www.luffscafe.com
Phone: 07815 202012

Coombe Cellars
Web: www.thecoombecellars.co.uk
Phone: 01626 872423

The Ness (Shaldon)
Web: www.theness.co.uk
Phone: 01626 873 480

Crab Shack
Web: www.crabshackonthebeach.co.uk
Phone: 01626 777 956

The Old Java Coffee House
Web: www.theoldjavacoffeehouse.co.uk
Phone: 01626 778526

The View Bar & Café
Web: www.theviewteignmouth.co.uk
Phone: 01626 249044

East Cliff Café
Web: www.facebook.com/EastCliffCafe/
Phone: 01626 777621

TwentySix
Web: www.twentysixcafe.co.uk
Phone: 01626 879000

Ye Olde Jolly Sailor Inn
Web: www.facebook.com/
YeOldeJollySailor/
Phone: 01626 772864

SELECTED ACCOMMODATION

Haytor Barns
Web: www.toadhallcottages.co.uk/
holiday-cottages/devon/dartmoor/haytor
Phone: 01548 20 20 20

Bramley Wood B&B
Web: www.bramblywood.co.uk
Phone: 01364 661474 or 07923 555587

The Edgemoor Hotel Dartmoor
Web: www.edgemoor.co.uk
Phone: 01626 832466

Cromwell Arms
Web: www.thecromwellarms.co.uk
Phone: 01626 833 473

Courtenay House - B&B
Web: www.courtenayhouse.co.uk
Phone: 01626 835363

Hazelwood Guest House
Web: www.hazelwoodguesthouse.com
Phone: 01626 366130

Premier Inn Newton Abbot
Web: https://www.premierinn.com/
gb/en/hotels/england/devon/newton-
abbot/newton-abbot.html
Phone: 0871 527 9300

The Thornhill B&B
Web: www.thethornhill.co.uk
Phone: 01626 773 460

Cliffden Hotel
Web: www.cliffdenhotel.com
Phone: 01626 770052

Lynton House Hotel
Web: www.lyntonhouseteignmouth.com
Phone: 01626 774349

Brunswick House B&B
Web: www.brunswick-house.com
Phone: 01626 774102

TAXIS

Haytor & Bovey Tracey

Mooreland Taxis
Phone: 01626 835095

Oakleigh Taxis
Phone: 07895 008289

Stover Taxis
Phone: 07546 469918

Newton Abbot

Gem's Taxi
Phone: 01626 201010

Station Taxis
01626 334488

Popton Taxi's
Phone: 07399 461049

Teignmouth

Alpha Taxis
Phone: 01626 773030

Kev's Taxis
Phone: 07803 577111

Aaztec Taxi's
Phone: 07474 027207

ADDITIONAL INFO

Devon Walking Trails
Web: www.devon.gov.uk/ddwalking.pdf

Shaldon Zoo
Web: www.shaldonwildlifetrust.org.uk
Phone: 01626 872234

Stover Country Park
Web: https://new.devon.gov.uk/
stovercountrypark/
Phone: 01626 835236

Pavilions Teignmouth
Web: www.pavilionsteignmouth.org.uk

Teignmouth Grand Pier
Web: www.teignmouthpier.com
Phone: 01626 774367

EMERGENCY SERVICES

Dartmoor Search and Rescue

If it is an emergency, dial 999 and ask for police.

Web: www.dsrtashburton.org.uk

Facebook: www.facebook.com/dartmoorrescueashburton

Twitter: @Dartmoor_SRTA

Email: info@ndsart.org.uk

RNLI Teignmouth

If it is an emergency, dial 999 and ask for Coastguard.

Web: www.teignmouthlifeboat.org.uk

Email: tonywatson@watsonlook.co.uk

Torbay Coastguard

If it is an emergency, dial 999 and ask for Coastguard.

Web: www.torbayhmcoastguard.co.uk

Facebook: @TorbayCoastguard

Twitter: @TorbayCRT

NOTES:

NOTES:

Printed in Great Britain
by Amazon